Just the Facts

LSD

Sean Connolly

Heinemann Library
Chicago, Illinois

Designed by M2 Graphic Design
Printed in Hong Kong / China
Originated by Ambassador Litho Ltd.

05 04 03 02 01
10 9 8 7 6 5 4 3 2

Library of Congress Cataloging-in-Publication Data
Connolly, Sean, 1956-
    LSD / Sean Connolly.
      p. cm. – (Just the facts)
    Includes bibliographical references and index.
    Summary: Discusses the history of the hallucinogenic drug LSD, its societal and physical effects, and where to go for help.
    ISBN 1-57572-258-5 (library)
    1. LSD (Drug)—Juvenile literature. [1. LSD (Drug) 2. Drug Abuse.] I. Title. II. Series.

RM666.L88 C66 2000
615'.7883—dc21   00-025655

Acknowledgments
The Publishers would like to thank the following for permission to reproduce photographs: Associated Press: pg.21; Bubbles: Pauline Cutter pg.32, Loisjoy Thurston pg.35, Pauline Cutter pg.39, Jennie Woodcock pg.44, Dr Hercules Robinson pg.49; David Hoffman: pg.8; Holt Studios: Nigel Cattlin pg.6, pg.7; Hulton Getty: pg.11, pg.15, pg.18; Impact: Eliza Armstrong pg.5, Mohamed Ansar pg.22, Peter Arkell pg.29; PA News: pg.25, pg.40; Photofusion: Liam Bailey pg.27; Retna: Jenny Acheson pg.51; Rex Features: pg.12, pg.17, pg.31, pg.37; Ronald Grant Archive: pg.9, pg.19; Science Photo Library: pg.34, pg.42, pg.47.

Cover photograph reproduced with permission of Science Photo Library.

Every effort has been made to contact copyright holders of any material reproduced in this book.
Any omissions will be rectified in subsequent printings if notice is given to the publisher.

Our special thanks to Pamela G. Richards, M.Ed., for her help in the preparation of the book.

Some words are shown in bold, **like this.** You can find out what they mean by looking in the glossary.

Contents

Introduction

LSD is the most common **hallucinogen,** as well as being one of the most **potent** drugs known to science. It takes only a microscopic amount of the drug to produce a powerful experience, or *trip,* which lasts up to twelve hours. During this trip, the LSD user encounters a bewildering array of images and sounds, sometimes jumbled together or exaggerated into strange distortions. Reality seems to recede into dim memory and is replaced with new sensations that rush through the mind. In addition, no two trips are identical. However, some of their effects can recur long after the trip is over in the form of **flashbacks.**

Myth and reality

Considering the power of LSD, it is not surprising that a number of conflicting claims have been made about it. Enthusiastic supporters believe it unlocks reserves of mental powers that can help worldwide understanding. Opponents of the drug have claimed that it can damage **chromosomes,** drive people crazy, or trigger mental illnesses such as **schizophrenia.**

Despite conflicting points of view, it would be foolish to rule out all aspects of the long- term consequences of using LSD. What is agreed is that we are still not aware of all there is to know about this powerful drug, or how it exerts such an effect on the brain.

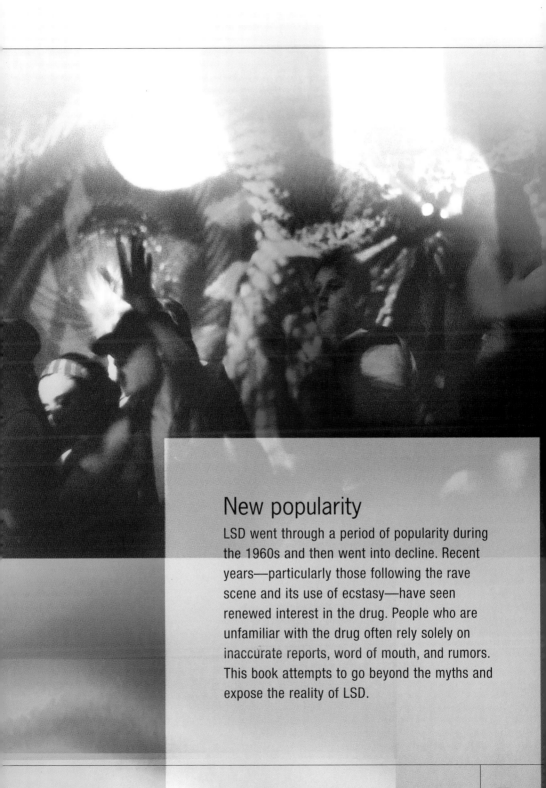

New popularity

LSD went through a period of popularity during the 1960s and then went into decline. Recent years—particularly those following the rave scene and its use of ecstasy—have seen renewed interest in the drug. People who are unfamiliar with the drug often rely solely on inaccurate reports, word of mouth, and rumors. This book attempts to go beyond the myths and expose the reality of LSD.

What Is LSD?

LSD is a **synthetic** substance manufactured from ergot, a **parasitic** fungus that grows naturally on rye and other grasses. The initials LSD stand for the chemical name of the substance, lysergic acid diethylamide. Another common name for the drug is *acid,* which refers to its chemical make-up. LSD is extremely powerful, and only a tiny amount has a **hallucinogenic** effect.

An LSD "trip"

LSD, which is odorless and colorless with a slightly bitter taste, has a powerful effect on the mind. After taking the drug, the user begins to experience the hallucinogenic effects known as a *trip.* The first effects begin about half an hour after taking the LSD; the effects peak about four to six hours later, and then fade after about eight to twelve hours. Unlike many other drugs, LSD produces very few physical changes; the pupils of the eyes **dilate** somewhat, and the body temperature rises slightly.

The actual experience of a trip is psychological. It differs from person to person, and even from time to time. Much depends on the mood of the person taking the drug and on the setting—whether he or she takes it alone or with a group of trusted friends. Most users perceive distorted shapes, intense colors, and even movement of stationary objects. There are also changes in hearing and in the sense of time and place. These changes in perception are usually described as **hallucinations,** although for the most part an LSD user knows that the changes are not real.

Helpless feelings

Although someone on an LSD trip is usually able to distinguish reality from drug-induced changes, these distortions can be upsetting and disturbing. Because there is no way of stopping a trip once it has started, the result can be a frightening experience called a *bad trip.* People who have this experience often report feelings of dizziness, anxiety, disorientation, and even **paranoia.**

The naturally occurring fungus ergot forms the basis for LSD, one of the most powerful of all mind-altering drugs. It grows on rye and other grasses.

Different trips

LSD is one of many drugs that people take for their **hallucinogenic** qualities. Some of these drugs are found naturally in plants that people collect. The closest effects to those of LSD come from psychedelic mushrooms, in which the active **compounds** psilocybin and psilocin react with the body's nervous system. The peyote cactus of North America contains mescaline, which also acts as a powerful **hallucinogen.** The trips from these plant-based drugs tend to be slightly shorter than an LSD trip, lasting about four hours.

Other hallucinogens are produced chemically. Some people take phencyclidine (PCP), also known as *angel dust,* in order to achieve an experience like that of an LSD trip. However, users often experience anxiety and panic.

Much of the LSD sold today comes in blotting paper strips with a logo on each dose.

Millions of doses

Chemically produced LSD is a white, odorless material that appears in crystal form. In this form, it is purchased in amounts weighing up to about 10 grams. Then the LSD is diluted into thousands or even millions of individual doses.

LSD is usually sold on the street by word of mouth. People exchange addresses and telephone numbers to ensure a steady supply. This unofficial network also links users with unofficial organizations that champion the use of LSD.

During the 1960s, widespread fear about LSD led to a series of shocking films.

The "Big Bang"

The **pharmaceutical** industry in the early decades of the twentieth century worked to isolate new drugs that could be used for medical purposes. Sandoz, a company based in Basel, Switzerland, had devoted much of its research to ergot, a type of fungus that grows on diseased kernels of rye. Ergot had been known as a folk medicine as long ago as the Middle Ages, when it was used as an aid in childbirth.

The first LSD trip

Albert Hofmann, the Sandoz scientist in charge of the ergot project, began **synthesizing molecules** of ergot during the mid-1930s. He worked carefully, noting each new **compound** and testing it on animals. Hofmann's goal was to find a drug that would cure painful conditions such as **migraines.** By 1943, he had reached the twenty-fifth compound with Lysergic Acid Diethylamide (LSD) as its base. The previous 24 compounds had had no effect on animals, so Hofmann took a tiny amount of LSD-25 himself. The result was astounding. Within half an hour, he was dizzy and laughing uncontrollably. As Hofmann rode his bicycle home, everything he saw and heard seemed distorted. Hofmann was experiencing the first LSD trip.

❝The dizziness and sensation of fainting became so strong at times that I could no longer hold myself erect. . . . My surroundings had now transformed themselves in more terrifying ways. Everything in the room spun around, and the familiar objects and pieces of furniture assumed grotesque, threatening forms.❞

(Albert Hofmann describing his LSD experience in *LSD: My Problem Child*)

Swiss chemist Albert Hofmann was one of the first people to recognize the significance of LSD.

Unknown powers

Hofmann had accidentally discovered one of the most powerful drugs ever developed. The following morning, however, he felt normal again—apart from a heightened appreciation of colors and sounds similar to his experience the previous night. Indeed, Hofmann was able to recall nearly everything that had occurred during his LSD experience. He concluded that he must have retained **consciousness** throughout.

As a trained scientist, Hofmann knew that his experience might have been a chance occurrence, so he wrote a report for the Sandoz research department that dealt with new discoveries. The company decided to test the drug in various doses on a wide range of animals. Each case revealed strange reactions. Spiders on a low dose of LSD wove incredibly complex webs; however, with higher doses did no weaving at all. Cats became very excited. A chimp was given LSD and put among other chimps. The result was chaos: the chimp on LSD ignored all the established colony social rules, and the other animals were completely confused. The Sandoz team knew that it had found a powerful drug, but had no real idea how it worked or what its effects on people might be.

Tool for psychology

The scientists eventually decided to test the drugs on human beings. Volunteers, including a psychiatrist associated with Sandoz, began to file a series of reports about their own experiences. One common reaction seemed to emerge. In low doses, LSD seemed to unleash memories that had long been **suppressed.** This news suggested that LSD might become a valuable aid in psychotherapy, a field of science that helped patients by allowing them to deal with their own memories. Among the conditions that LSD was said to cure were **schizophrenia,** criminal behavior, and **alcoholism.** It was at this stage that Sandoz began recommending that psychologists take LSD themselves "to gain an understanding of the **subjective** experiences of the schizophrenic." Following this advice, many college psychology students took the drug.

Throughout the 1950s, psychologists used LSD to relax patients and to unleash their memories. They also took the drug to help them understand how the patients themselves felt. Psychologists in the United States used LSD to treat alcohol and drug addiction. The drug was also used on terminally ill patients to ease pain and help them face death. But most of all, psychologists valued the way LSD could release buried memories. The U.S. military viewed LSD as a drug that could potentially disable an army without the use of weapons.

Film star Cary Grant was one of the high-profile people who took LSD as part of psychological therapy during the 1950s.

The LSD Industry

When Sandoz Laboratories began developing LSD during the 1940s, the company soon realized that it had developed the most powerful **hallucinogenic** substance in the world. Albert Hofmann's initial caution about the dosages was well founded. Dosages of LSD are measured in micrograms, or millionths of a gram. By comparison, dosages of heroin and cocaine are measured in milligrams, or thousandths of a gram. LSD is said to be 100 times more **potent** than the hallucinogenic drug psilocybin and 4,000 times stronger than mescaline. Both psilocybin and mescaline were treated with caution before LSD arrived on the scene.

Looking for benefits

At first, Sandoz tried unsuccessfully to find a medical use for the new drug; LSD did not work as a **stimulant** to the **respiratory** or circulatory systems. The experiences of Hofmann and several other human test subjects, however, sent researchers looking into the area with which LSD would be tied for nearly six decades—the human mind.

By 1947, Sandoz had begun producing LSD in large enough amounts to be sold commercially. They gave the drug the name *Delysid* and **marketed** it as a psychological cure-all.

Henry Luce Robinson was the co-founder of the American weekly news magazine *Time.* A fervent anti-Communist, he is known to have taken LSD at a time when some scientists believed it was a mind-enhancing drug.

Powerful suppliers

During the late 1940s, other companies also began producing large quantities of LSD. They too emphasized the powerful psychological effects of the new drug. Soon LSD gained the reputation as the drug associated with the highly educated. After all, it had been developed by a trained research chemist and popularized by high-ranking members of the psychological community. Unlike other drugs, such as marijuana, which start out being popular with the general population and then working through the upper classes, LSD began as a creation of the highly trained and worked down to the general population. More and more people learned of its existence, largely because the people who used it spread the word through lectures and educational articles.

Among the groups that became interested in LSD were the military and **intelligence** communities. They saw the drug as a psychological tool and weapon. In the 1950s, the U.S. Central Intelligence Agency (CIA) began twenty years of tests on LSD.

CIA officials saw LSD as a way of both **demoralizing** an enemy and reversing the effects of **brainwashing.** Tests were carried out on prisoners taken during the Korean War and on American soldiers. Prompting these tests was the hope that the drug, so far hailed as a powerful memory tool, would become a powerful weapon.

The wider arena

Although the military carried out many of these experiments itself, using its own supplies of LSD, it turned to leading universities for more detailed studies. By the late 1950s, the academic studies took on a different tone, and the flow of LSD increased. "Captain" Al Hubbard, a former American spy, bought a vast amount of LSD from Sandoz and distributed it among his friends in the fields of art, industry, science, and even religion. Two psychologists at Harvard University, Timothy Leary and Richard Alpert, were in a good position to observe and document the new trends.

Many of the military tests were carried out at Harvard and, in addition, the two men moved in the circles where people had been offered some of Hubbard's supplies. They quickly turned their attention to the newly created field of "**psychedelic** research" and made many friends who would help them spread the popularity of LSD. One of the most famous was British writer Aldous Huxley, who had long been a champion of research into the inner workings of the human mind.

The shifting lights of psychedelic rock shows, with music by bands such as the Grateful Dead (above), echoed the experience of an LSD trip.

❝All my thoughts centered on death. I felt like I was in the middle of a psychadelic hurricane with no way out.❞

(Anonymous user describing a bad trip)

Power to the People?

Timothy Leary's involvement with LSD kicked off the 1960s, a decade highly associated with the drug. The underground LSD industry also developed during that time.

With Leary and Alpert as champions of the cause for LSD, word spread rapidly. Many young people were tempted by the promises of expanded **consciousness** and inner fulfillment. On the other hand, the authorities felt threatened by these promises, as well as the so-called research that backed them. Leary and Alpert lost their Harvard teaching positions in 1963. However, at about the same time, another charismatic leader arrived on the scene to promote LSD.

Author Ken Kesey (left) encouraged many people to take LSD. His book *One Flew over the Cuckoo's Nest* (a scene from the film version with Jack Nicholson is shown right) was inspired by his own experiences as an LSD "guinea pig."

Mad scientists?

On the East Coast, Leary and Alpert represented the traditional, scientific approach to researching LSD; however, other unconventional methods emerged. On the West Coast of the United States, Ken Kesey was fast becoming the spokesman for LSD. Kesey was a young author who had written two highly praised novels, including the famous *One Flew over the Cuckoo's Nest*. Like Alpert and Leary, Kesey had taken LSD and believed that the public should share the secret.

Because Kesey did not operate within the procedures of academic science, he based his LSD experiments on recreation or pleasure. Throughout 1964 and 1965, when LSD was still legal and in plentiful supply, Kesey assembled a group of young people eager to test the new drug in nearly every circumstance possible. The group became known as "the Merry Pranksters" and lived up to its name by attracting hundreds of people to LSD parties across California. Some of these parties, much like today's raves, featured large bowls of punch spiked with drugs. At that time, however, the drug used was LSD.

The crackdown

Following the efforts of Kesey and similar LSD advocates in the United States and other countries, use of the drug increased dramatically during the mid-1960s. Meanwhile, disturbing reports of the drug's power emerged. By 1966, the public outcry became very loud. The United States became the first of many countries to outlaw the drug.

By 1968, LSD was no longer prescribed for the few remaining psychological conditions it was meant to treat. From that time forward, the whole LSD industry went **underground.** A select group of scientists, however, had studied the complex formulas needed to produce the drug. These so-called *cooks* produced large enough amounts of LSD to supply all of the United States; similar cooks were at work in Europe. Cooks guarded their formulas closely. They occasionally passed the formula down to others, but mostly limited production to a very small band of individuals.

This system has continued for more than 30 years. Even now, drug-control officials estimate that fewer than a dozen cooks produce all of the LSD distributed in the United States. Similar LSD-producing societies exist in other countries.

The LSD guru

The name Timothy Leary crops up again and again in discussions about the history and significance of LSD. Leary, who was born in Massachusetts in 1920, was the first person to build a wide public stage for the drug. Leary's experiments, which were conducted in scientific surroundings during the early 1960s, seemed to promise miracles from the powerful drug. In 1966, Leary formed a **psychedelic** religion called the League for Spiritual Discovery. Leary found investors for his research center in Millbrook, New York. However, when LSD became illegal, Leary was arrested some ten times before seeking **asylum** in Switzerland. He was sent back to the United States in 1973 and spent three years in prison. After his release in 1976, Leary turned away from drugs and began to speak about the power of the communication revolution. Throughout the 1980s, Leary wrote books and computer software; his lectures now focused on computer technology and the Internet. Leary died of prostate cancer in 1996.

"If you can remember the sixties, you weren't there."

(Popular saying, referring to the widespread use of LSD and other drugs)

Who Takes LSD?

Many people believe that fashion moves in cycles. Clothing, furniture, and music that are scorned in one decade reappear as high fashion only a few years later. During the 1990s, it became acceptable to appreciate things from the 1960s. Feature films such as *Austin Powers, International Man of Mystery* and *Lost in Space* celebrated sixties culture; groups such as Oasis and Kula Shaker recalled the Beatles; and even the word *cool* regained popularity.

The trip continues

Even as people in the 1990s made gentle fun of the 1960s, there were several important similarities between the decades. One major link was a reemerging interest in the so-called **counterculture.** While during the 1960s young people rebelled against the stifling attitudes of the 1950s, during the 1990s many young people turned their backs on the perceived selfishness of the 1980s. This attitude was reflected in the popularity of books about spirituality.

Spiritual pursuits such as meditation, like the renewed popularity of LSD, are links to the enduring legacy of the 1960s.

These trends meant that the time was ripe for the return of a drug claiming to promise increased self-awareness. Like they were 30 years ago, many LSD users today are convinced that the drug is a gateway to greater understanding and empathy.

The party scene

Spurring LSD use today is the rave culture, or dance scene. During raves, or all-night dance parties, many young people take the drug ecstasy and dance all night. Because LSD has similar qualities, it too has become part of the scene.

Widening appeal

When LSD first became relatively widespread during the 1960s, it appealed mainly to people in their late teens and early twenties. However, surveys taken during the 1990s showed that many younger people were experimenting with the drug. A 1997 U.S. survey showed that nearly 8.5 percent of high-school seniors have tried LSD.

The Lure of LSD

The memory jolt provided by LSD is a powerful attraction for some people. Others enjoy the sensations of "hearing colors" and "seeing sounds," or the perceived movement of patterns on wallpaper or paintings. The term *trip* arose when some of the first LSD users referred to their experience as "a trip inside the mind." Although the experience varies, regular users say they sense a feeling of heightened self-awareness. They may also feel that their trip has a **mystical** or spiritual element.

Open to suggestions

An LSD user who experiences feelings of grandeur and keen sensitivity probably started the trip expecting some sort of **enlightenment.** Likewise, someone experiencing a bad trip probably started out feeling anxious. These experiences point to the basic **contradiction** of LSD: although the effects of a single trip are unpredictable, the overall experience depends greatly on surroundings and emotional state.

British police seized this load of LSD in 1978. It contained enough LSD for 670,000 doses and had a street value of $1.5 million. This value would be much higher by today's prices.

Blotters, sheets, or tablets

The tiny amounts of LSD needed for a trip are astounding. Only 300 millionths of a gram are enough to produce a twelve-hour trip. To be sold on the street, these tiny doses are usually mixed with alcohol and absorbed onto small pieces of blotting paper. This preparation is named *blotter acid* after the blotting paper used. The paper is often decorated with various designs. LSD is less commonly available in gelatin sheets, sugar cubes, or in tablets or capsules.

Where Is LSD Found?

Despite its reputation for sending each user on a personal, hair-raising, psychological journey, LSD tends to be taken in groups. When LSD first hit the headlines during the 1960s, it was associated with hippie culture. At concerts, music festivals, or small house parties, people usually took LSD together.

Much of the hippie peace-and-love sensibility arose from the responsibility of helping fellow drug users avoid unsettling experiences. For hippies, life was about peace and harmony and, above all, sharing. In fact, the idea of taking LSD alone was seen as selfish. Modern users share many of these views, even if hippie culture has become social history.

The risks

Although many LSD users scoff at stories of suicides or insanity attributed to a single use of acid, there are many circumstances in which LSD is very dangerous. People who use small amounts of other drugs, such as alcohol, cocaine, or amphetamines, believe that they can still concentrate on most tasks. However, LSD is different; it immediately dominates the brain, making it almost impossible to perform any task that requires concentration. Driving a car or operating machinery can be suicide for someone on an LSD trip.

Still rolling

In 1964, Ken Kesey's Merry Pranksters toured the United States in a brightly painted bus, taking LSD, playing musical instruments, and making hours of films. They organized concerts in California, where tubs of soft drinks were laced with LSD. Kesey was later arrested and spent time in prison. In the 1990s, Kesey and a new generation of Merry Pranksters were still advocating cutting loose from society. However, they were no longer recommending LSD as the fuel for the trip.

The LSD Scene

Even a person who acknowledges **dependence** on alcohol still thinks he or she can still manage to work, at least over the short term. The same is true for users of amphetamines, marijuana, and cocaine. In each case, the effects of the drug wear off after a few hours, leaving the user free to do other things.

The time commitment

However, the situation of a regular LSD user is different. There is no way to mix LSD with a normal routine. The LSD trip becomes not just the most important element in the user's day, but the only element. Someone who has just taken LSD will be virtually rooted to the spot for the next twelve hours. Driving a car is out of the question, and the hallucinations associated with the drug make such daily activities as catching a bus assume nightmarish proportions.

Typical LSD users take the drug in the late afternoon or early evening, depending on the setting. The drug is usually taken earlier if the person is staying inside with friends, or later at a more public festival or rave. After about half an hour, the trip takes over and the LSD user has no choice but to stay put and ride it out.

The setting

Most people take LSD in a group, preferably among people they know and trust. There are few experiences more upsetting than a bad trip, so regular users count on the support of friends around them. These familiar, or at least pleasant, surroundings make up what most LSD users refer to as the *setting*.

The small group that has taken LSD is quiet for about the first half hour, then giggles and muted laughter take over. The drug has begun to take effect. It is no exaggeration to describe the next twelve hours as a psychological roller-coaster ride, with mood changes often accompanying a dazzling array of images flashing before the eyes. Typically, the trip leaves the user with a profound sense of fatigue.

Regular use of LSD could cause someone to leave school at a time when young people should be maturing and building friendships.

A slacker's drug?

LSD is usually associated with young people without major responsibilities. A closer examination reveals why this may be true. The length of an LSD trip is one obvious factor: no one working hard at school or a steady job could possibly combine the LSD experience with a disciplined routine. Secondly, there is the trip itself. A mature adult drinker can use alcohol in **moderation;** however, there is no such thing as moderation where LSD is involved. The very nature of the LSD experience blots out the real world and sends users into themselves.

LSD has been used **recreationally** for more than three decades, and there are many similarities among the people who have taken it over the years. Extensive studies in the United States indicate that the average LSD user is male and in his late teens or early twenties. Although the percentage of young men who have taken LSD has risen within this group, the trend does not seem to have spread beyond that.

Getting ahold of LSD

Because it is so concentrated, LSD can be produced in huge quantities at very little cost. Once someone has learned of it, usually by word of mouth, LSD is easy to buy. It is compact and easy to conceal. These factors, plus the low cost of the drug, mean that LSD can easily gain a dangerous foothold in the community.

Not so safe

Many LSD users argue that scary stories about the drug are not based on truth. They can also show that other drugs such as cocaine cause as many as forty times more hospital emergencies than LSD does. Nevertheless, LSD casualties are concentrated among a younger, narrower, age group: in 1993, LSD ranked fourth in the United States as a cause of medical emergencies, after alcohol/drug combinations, marijuana, and cocaine.

Family and Friends

Unlike longtime users of amphetamines, alcohol, or heroin, people who use LSD do not regularly display any physical signs of the activity. At home they might be inclined to sleep a bit later, but the rest of the family would probably assume that this was caused by very late nights. Real changes would become obvious only if they were to start taking the drug during the week. Then the missed school, fatigue, and lack of **motivation** would stand out.

Effects on friendships

Usually, friends have a better idea of what is going on among people in their own group. Apart from learning through the grapevine that someone was taking acid, they would soon recognize the changes. For many drug users, taking LSD is seen as crossing a threshold. Even if there is less of a **stigma** attached to taking LSD among young people than there is among their parents, they still recognize that it is an intensely powerful drug. Many people are concerned about being drawn in, through **peer pressure**, to a threatening world of psychological experimentation. At the same time, LSD users often delude themselves into thinking that non-users lead dull lives, and as a result might abandon friendships. Also, non-users cannot connect emotionally or psychologically with friends who are tripping on LSD. These conditions push many friendships beyond the breaking point.

New Directions

A small handful of dried *magic mushrooms*, *left*, can produce an experience like that of an LSD trip.

After its decline during the 1970s and return to popularity during the 1990s, LSD has become both plentiful and cheap. Considering **inflation,** the drug is probably less expensive than it ever was. Most people pay about $2–5 for a hit, or single dose. Unlike the underground LSD **market** of the 1960s, today's market seems more commercial.

The hard-nosed business values of the 1980s are evident in the way LSD is sold today. Blank sheets of blotting paper have been replaced with tabs that appear to have been produced by a major company. Even the **logos** on the tabs have a more sophisticated look. They include such well-known images as Bart Simpson or Saddam Hussein.

Today, people take LSD for different reasons as well. Thirty years ago, people took LSD to contemplate eternal mysteries, and larger doses seemed to provide the key. Today, a typical tab contains about 50 micrograms of the drug, about one-fifth of the 1960s dosage.

Gateway drug?

For many young people, ecstasy is often a bridge to LSD. The LSD experience, in turn, leads some people to other **hallucinogenic** drugs, either because they think they are more "natural," or because they provide a different experience. These drugs range from DMT, LSD's powerful chemical cousin, to Cloud 9, which is promoted as a supposedly safe, all-natural version of ecstasy. Various types of mushroom, especially the psilocybe or so-called "magic mushroom," produce effects that are similar to those of LSD but last only about four hours. The mushroom "trip" is the effect caused by the mushroom poisoning the body.

LSD and Addiction

Several medical texts define addiction as "the repetitive, compulsive use of a substance that occurs despite negative consequences to the user." This definition further distinguishes between two types of **dependence,** physical and psychological. Heroin and alcohol are good examples of drugs that produce a physical dependence. In each case, the dependent feels an overwhelming compulsion to have the drug, sometimes just to feel "normal" again. Using this criteria, LSD cannot be said to lead to physical dependence.

Psychological dependence and LSD

Psychological dependence is an altogether different and more complicated issue. An LSD user doesn't need the drug in quite the same way that an alcoholic needs alcohol as a crutch to deal with all sorts of social occasions. The LSD user often feels a sense of sadness when coming down from his or her trip. The person psychologically dependent on LSD imagines that this sadness, which seems to be linked with returning to the ordinary, routine world, is reduced by taking LSD again.

Taking LSD for several days in a row, whether to avoid the sense of sadness and loss associated with stopping the drug or simply to experience an extended trip, clearly leads to **tolerance** to the drug. Tolerance is often considered part of the cycle of addiction and dependence. Even on the second day of a long LSD trip, an LSD user needs to take a much higher dose than the day before to achieve the same level of experience.

People who use LSD often adopt lifestyles that reject the accepted standards of consumer society. They may scorn "normal" work or study and advertise their drug-induced sensibilities through their clothes, music, artwork, and even automobiles.

Echoes of Terror

Many LSD supporters argue that the terrors of a bad trip end after the effects of the drug have worn off; however, the psychological effects of a bad trip can linger for some time afterward. Many people have reported feelings of depression, loss of confidence, instability, and **paranoia** after using LSD. The effects are magnified for those who are already psychologically vulnerable, such as people suffering from **schizophrenia** or other mental-health conditions. Some psychologists believe that LSD might hasten—if not exactly cause—the development of schizophrenia in some people.

> **"LSD is not a party drug. If you treat it like one, you're bound to get in trouble."**
>
> **(Steve Hager, magazine editor)**

Flashbacks

One of the most puzzling aspects about LSD is the experience of **flashbacks,** which can occur occasionally for several years after someone last takes LSD. During a flashback, some of the **hallucinogenic** elements of the last LSD trip suddenly reappear for a few minutes. Many users are alarmed by the rapid and completely unexpected distortion of their surroundings. Some studies indicate that up to 77 percent of LSD users have flashbacks.

Although flashbacks are unpredictable, they seem to be triggered most often by anxiety, fatigue, moving about in darkness, or smoking marijuana. Because flashbacks are, in effect, echoes of the last LSD experience, they can sometimes resemble a bad trip. Also, a person who has a bad trip while deliberately taking LSD can usually call on friends for support; however, they are often left stranded alone during a disturbing flashback.

❝I have previously taken LSD on four occasions. The first occasion I had a bad trip, and on the third and fourth occasions I got flashbacks from the previous trip, experiencing the same effects.❞

(Anonymous respondents to an Ohio State University survey about LSD use)

Legal Matters

The United States classifies LSD as a Class I drug. It is illegal to possess, distribute, or manufacture LSD. In the United States, a person caught trafficking LSD for the first time can be sentenced from 5 to 40 years in prison and fined up to $2 million. For a second offense, the penalty is much stiffer: from ten years to life in prison and a fine ranging between $4 and $10 million.

Police officers display LSD ingredients found hidden in a packet of dog food.

Zero tolerance policies

Many schools around the United States have adopted zero tolerance policies in regard to drugs and other dangerous activities. If a student is found with drugs or weapons, he or she can be immediately expelled. Such zero tolerance policies are also used in many places of business and in professional sports organizations.

Controlled Substance Act

The Controlled Substances Act (CSA), Title II of the Comprehensive Drug Abuse Prevention and Control Act of 1970, is the legal foundation of the United States government's fight against the abuse of drugs and other substances. This law is a consolidation of many laws regulating the manufacture and distribution of narcotics, stimulants, depressants, hallucinogens, steroids, and chemicals used in the unlawful production of controlled substances.

Raw ingredients

LSD is commonly produced from lysergic acid, which itself is made from ergotamine tartrate, a substance found on an ergot fungus on rye grain. These raw ingredients are controlled by anti-drugs laws in most countries. In the United States, for example, lysergic acid and lysergic acid amide are regulated under the Controlled Substances Act; ergotamine tartrate is regulated under the Chemical Diversion and Trafficking Act.

Life with LSD

The experience of taking LSD can be divided into two stages: the actual LSD trip and the long-term changes to the user's personality after taking the drug. Although a person tripping on LSD will not see anything that isn't really there, the drug has enormous potential to change the senses and emotions. The changes come rapidly and unexpectedly, often leaving the user in a state of panic and disorientated confusion.

Carrying on

Although LSD does not produce physical **dependence,** an occasional user might become attracted to the same set of circumstances that led to his or her first trip. This could mean entering more fully into the rave scene or seeking out other places where LSD is likely to be used.

The negative side-effects of LSD are also related to the power of the drug. A single bad trip is often enough to turn someone off LSD, and the possibility of **flashbacks** often reinforce this decision. A small number of people, however, have thrown themselves wholly into the world of **psychedelic**

experiences. Such people might use LSD more than several times a week as well as experiment with a wide range of other **hallucinatory** drugs. It is among these users that the casualties of LSD are found. Such people seem to live in the altered reality of the LSD experience, whether or not they have taken the drug. They find it hard to concentrate, to study, or to keep a job that involves attention to detail. The fuzzy grip on reality demonstrated by such LSD users proves the potential harm of the drug.

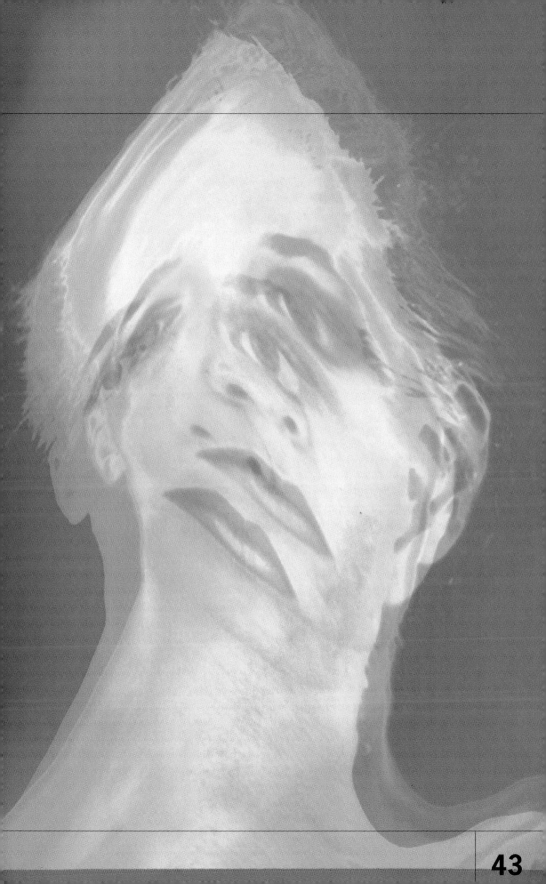

Calling it quits

It need not take a bad trip or a series of disconcerting **flashbacks** to persuade someone to stop taking LSD. Some people recognize the fact that ultimately the "truths" they discover are based on chemical reactions in the brain. Regardless of their varied experiences, they finally feel that enough is enough.

❝I might never use it again or not for a long time, if ever. The reason is that I am a nervous person to begin with and it was aggravated.❞

(Anonymous respondent to the Ohio State University survey on LSD use)

"In almost the same breath you will feel elated, scared, wonderful, ridiculous— part of the universal hoax, and then all these swirling certainties and uncertainties will break into fragments and begin and end again."

(Anonymous respondent to the Ohio State University survey on LSD use, describing the experience of a trip)

Treatment and Counseling

LSD is a special case when compared to many other drugs of abuse. It does not produce a damaging **dependence,** it is rarely linked to violence, and it does not encourage the user to resort to crime. The picture, however, is by no means rosy. LSD produces terrifying effects in both the short and long term, and it has been linked to permanent psychological damage.

Natural controls

Although LSD produces more dramatic psychological effects than nearly any other drug, there are certain factors that seem to prevent a damaging decline in the user's mental or physical health. Drug workers refer to the factors that keep the use of LSD in check as **governors.** LSD produces a high level of **tolerance** after only several uses in quick succession; the user finds no benefit in taking the drug too often. This tolerance cannot be overcome by taking larger doses. Two other factors act as governors to prevent frequent abuse of LSD. The first is the length of the experience

itself. With trips lasting up to twelve hours, the user is unlikely to need to buy the drug very frequently. This comparatively rare use contrasts with amphetamines and—especially— crack, drugs that abusers need to buy repeatedly and frequently to regain the feeling of a high. Finally, the unpredictable nature of an LSD trip limits the amount of times that people take the drug. After an LSD experience, the user feels disorientated and needs time to settle. A bad trip is often enough to persuade a user to stop taking LSD.

Restoring calm

It is important to know what to do if you encounter someone suffering from a bad LSD trip. Drug workers call the fearful effects of a bad trip "acute panic reactions." Reassurance is vital, along with calm persuasion that things will work out. The first thing to do is to reassure the person that he or she is not going to die or go crazy, and that what the person is feeling is the result of the drug.

It is important to take the person somewhere quiet and not leave him or her alone. If qualified medical help is not available, one or two friends should remain close by to keep the person calm. Don't use any type of restraint; this would only reinforce the person's sense of panic. Once the person is at a hospital, doctors who learn of any previous mental health problems will insist on making a thorough examination before releasing him or her.

The San Francisco LSD scene

In the United States, the undisputed center of the LSD movement was San Francisco. The city was home to such drug-influenced events as the "Human Be-In" and "Summer of Love." Teeming with tens of thousands of tripping hippies, the city's Haight-Ashbury district became what historian Jay Stevens called "a kind of sanitarium . . . that offered a therapeutic regime of good vibes and drugs, rather than mountain air and mineral springs." Eventually, LSD-related suicides, caused by tripping young people wandering into traffic or through plate-glass windows, convinced adults that something very disturbing was happening.

❝I found a counselor who talked to me about the problems with my family and other things, and gradually the flashbacks wore off. They were so frightening, sometimes they'd last for six or eight hours. The thought of drugs or alcohol really scares me now.❞

(Tanya, age 16, discussing the lasting effects of a bad trip in *Drug Wise*)

People to Talk To

LSD has been a source of wonder, confusion, and fear for more than 50 years. Along the way, people have said it could change the world into a better place overnight, or that it would make first-time users insane. It is important to ignore rumor and hearsay in favor of scientific data and sensible first-hand accounts by people familiar with the drug.

Friendly advice

Parents, teachers, and youth workers are the first people to ask for information about LSD. However, many young people are afraid to approach these people. There are also drug-awareness organizations that provide information about drugs as well as help to people with drug problems. With LSD, one of the biggest problems is getting reliable information in a confidential setting.

The United States has a wide range of organizations where young people can find out more about the effects of alcohol and other drugs. They provide confidential or even free telephone advice, or they can suggest local agencies throughout the United States. Some groups are geared specifically towards young people.

Whether you approach one of these organizations or a family member, a youth leader, or teacher, it is important to discuss your concerns openly.

Practical details

Helplines and drug organizations can offer practical advice on a number of aspects of LSD that are rarely mentioned. For example, LSD is a fragile chemical that can easily turn to lysergic salt when warmed. Lysergic salt can cause acute stomach cramps. Being able to identify such pains can be helpful if you are dealing with someone who is terrified by these effects. Helpline volunteers are also well suited to describe the effects of mixing LSD with other drugs, and this knowledge can be helpful if someone is struggling through a bad trip.

Information and Advice

The United States and many other countries are well served by organizations that provide advice, counseling, and other information relating to drug use. The contacts listed on these pages are helpful springboards for obtaining such advice or for providing confidential information over the telephone or by mail.

Drug awareness contacts

Center for Substance Abuse Prevention
5600 Fishers Lane, Rockwall II
Rockville, MD 20857
(301) 443-0365

Child Welfare League of America
440 First Street NW
Washington, DC 20001
(202) 638-2952
The Child Welfare League of America, based in Washington, provides useful contacts across the country in most areas relating to young people's problems, many of them related to drug involvement.

DARE America
PO Box 775
Dumfries, VA 22026
(703) 860-3273
Drug Abuse Resistance and Education (DARE) America is a national organization that links law-enforcement and educational resources to provide up-to-date and comprehensive information about all aspects of drug use.

Just Say No International
2000 Franklin St., Suite 400
Oakland, CA 94612-2908

National Institute on Drug Abuse
6001 Executive Blvd.
Bethesda, MD 20892-9561
(301) 443-1124

Partnership for a Drug-Free America
405 Lexington Ave., 16th floor
New York, NY 10174
(212) 922-1560

Students Against Drugs and Alcohol (SADA)
7443 E. 68th St.
Tulsa, OK 74133
(918) 249-1315

Youth Power
300 Lakeside Drive
Oakland, CA 94612
(510) 451-6666, Ext. 24
Youth Power is a nationwide organization involved in widening awareness of drug-related problems. It sponsors clubs and local affiliates across the country in an effort to help young people make their own sensible choices about drugs, and to work against the negative effects of peer pressure.

More Books to Read

Grosshandler-Smith, Janet. Edited by Ruth C. Rosen. *Drugs and the Law*. New York, N.Y.: The Rosen Publishing Group, Inc., 1997.

Jaffe, Steven L., ed. Introduction by Barry R. McCaffrey. *How to Get Help*. Broomall, Pa.: Chelsea House Publishers, 1999.

Kuhn, Cynthia, and Scott Swartzwelder. *Buzzed.* New York, N.Y.: W.W. Norton and Company, 1998.

Littell, Mary A. *LSD*. Berkeley Heights, N.J.: Enslow Publishers, Inc., 1996.

Mass, Wendy. *Teen Drug Abuse*. San Diego, Calif.: Lucent Books, 1997.

Monroe, Judy. *LSD, PCP and Hallucinogen Drug Dangers*. Berkeley Heights, N.J.: Enslow Publishers, Inc., 2000.

Salak, John. *Drugs in Society: Are They Our Suicide Pill?* Brookfield, Conn.: Twenty-First Century Books, Inc., 1995.

Trulson, Michael E. *LSD: Visions or Nightmares?* Broomall, Pa.: Chelsea House Publishers, 1985.

Glossary

alcoholism disease linked to a dependence on alcohol

asylum place offering safety or shelter

brainwashing using psychological methods, including drugs, to alter someone's memory

chromosomes elements in human cells that pass on inherited characteristics

compound combination of two or more elements or parts

consciousness state of being awake and aware of one's surroundings

contradiction statement that is inconsistent with itself or with other statements

counterculture culture, especially of young people, with values or lifestyles in opposition to those of the established culture

demoralizing causing someone to lose confidence

dependence physical or psychological craving for something, such as a drug

dilate make larger or wider

enlightenment gaining in understanding, the solution to difficult problems

flashback element of an LSD trip that recurs, sometimes long after the effects of the drug have worn off

governor factor that acts to control behavior

hallucinations images that people think they see, but are not really there

hallucinogen substance that produces hallucinations

hallucinogenic able to produce hallucinations

inflation tendency for prices to rise so that the same amount of money decreases in value as time goes by

intelligence branch of government that deals with gathering information and spying

kaleidoscopic having a bewildering array of moving bright colors

logo design or emblem associated with a product

market advertise and distribute a product widely

migraine severe headache, often associated with disturbed vision, that lasts for a long time

moderation state of not being excessive

molecule tiny collection of atoms

motivation urge to work harder or to improve oneself

mystical having a mysterious or spiritual nature

paranoia belief that everyone is against you

parasitic related to parasitism, or living off another creature

peer pressure pressure from friends of the same age to behave in a certain way

pharmaceutical relating to drugs

potent having a powerful effect

psychedelic relating generally to hallucinations, or specifically to the LSD experience

recreationally with no medical reason, for fun

respiratory relating to the lungs and breathing

schizophrenia psychological condition characterized by mental confusion and sometimes associated with hearing voices

stigma mark of disgrace or stain on a person's character

stimulant drug that excites the body or the mind

subjective as experienced by an individual rather than expressed generally

suppressed kept out of the immediate memory

synthetic produced by people, often in a laboratory or factory

tolerance way the body learns to expect more of a substance, such as a drug

underground out of sight of authorities, especially from the police or other law enforcement agencies

Index